Never Drink
Coffee from Your
Saucer...

AND OTHER TIPS ON
SOCIALLY CORRECT DINING

Never Drink Coffee from Your Saucer...

AND OTHER TIPS ON SOCIALLY CORRECT DINING

Sheila M. Long

ANDREWS AND McMEEL

A UNIVERSAL PRESS SYNDICATE COMPANY

KANSAS CITY

Library of Congress Cataloging-in-Publication Data
Long, Sheila M.
    Never drink coffee from your saucer : --and other tips on socially correct
dining / by Sheila M. Long.
        p.   cm.
    ISBN 0-8362-2169-9 (pbk.)
    1. Table etiquette. 2. Dinners and dining 3. Entertaining.
    I. Title.
    BJ2041.L658   1996
    395'.54--dc20

                                                        96-23797
                                                           CIP

This book is dedicated to the following women in my life:

My grandmothers, Cookie Mae and Grannie Vie.

Cookie Mae enlightened me on correct dining etiquette and constantly reminded me that "You cannot have two sets of manners."

Grannie Vie, at age 100, still educates all her family members on the "proper way to dine."

Honey, my mother, who with a glance can register approval.

Aunts Rita and Dot, who started my sterling silver when I was only ten years old and who continue to enlighten me.

Contents

1

A place setting for dinner.
Explanations of silverware, dinnerware, and
   glassware.

2

What to do before, during, and after dining.
How to eat certain foods.
Solutions to common blunders.

3

**HOW TO BE A GRACIOUS HOST
OR HOSTESS**

Preparation before entertaining.

Dinner is served:

What to do during the meal.

Hints for the host and hostess.

4

**DINING AND ENTERTAINING AT
RESTAURANTS**

How to entertain at a restaurant.

General etiquette for dining at restaurants.

5

**DINING AT MEETINGS, PARTIES,
AND LUXURIOUS PLACES**

Conducting business meetings while dining.

Types of parties.

Luxurious places for dining.

Acknowledgments

The following book became a collaboration of many people's conversations about dining problems and situations. Writing this book was hard work, and the contributions of the following team members helped bring a book of this quality to print.

I am grateful to my husband, Patrick, whose encouragement and laughter spirited all of us through this brisk undertaking. His vision and sense of humor kept us focused on what is important in life: "Have fun while working, no matter what."

Our sons, Kevin and Vincent, gave me the perspective of the twentysomething generation and provided me with lively discussions of what topics should be included.

My father, John Henry Armstrong, pointed out humorous elements of etiquette that only a father could tell an author/daughter.

Heather Boustany provided smiles, encouragement, development of text, and many rewrites. Her vitality pushed everyone beyond their limits.

The editing was executed to perfection with the calm demeanor and brilliance of Rose Batson. How she incorporated my many rewrites was a miracle.

The text was reviewed for its technical accuracy by Barry Whitten who trained at the Ritz-Carlton and is the Food and Beverage Director at the exclusive Austin Club in Austin, Texas.

The illustrations by Mike Krone added just the right touch. He always understood the exact feeling that I wanted to convey.

Introduction

This little book grew out of a 1990s dilemma and a genteel memory. The dilemma is the hectic pace of our lives, which has created the need for quick references on everything. The memory comes from my sweet but firm grandmother, who constantly reminded me, "You can't have two sets of manners—one for home and the other for show!"

Her admonition taught me that good manners matter in every setting and that regardless of how rushed our lives become, we need a little gentility. In fact, the lack of it can quickly derail a fast-track career.

In my work as a corporate trainer, I see employees passed over for promotions, salary increases, and new jobs because they lack essential social graces. This shortcoming becomes especially evident when it involves dining etiquette, because business often entails eating out or entertaining.

Knowing the correct dining etiquette gives you more confidence so you can relax and enjoy social gatherings, no matter how formal. Entertaining around the dining table can promote both business and friendship.

I wrote this book as a concise reference for busy people who have little spare time and who want to spend that time enjoying life to its fullest. The book is organized to be quick and easy to read. Its compact size fits easily into your briefcase or purse so you can always have it at your fingertips.

Despite its small size, *Never Drink Coffee from Your Saucer* contains all the essential guidelines about how to conduct yourself in any dining situation, including how to use silverware and glassware, how to dine formally and informally, how to eat certain foods, and how to avoid common etiquette mistakes.

This concise, handy reference will let you think of dining, whether as guest, host, or hostess, with confidence and enthusiasm. Bon Appetit!

Sheila M. Long

1

Introduction to a Place Setting

This section illustrates and discusses:

- A table setting, including silverware, dinner-ware, and glassware
- Each piece of silverware, where it is placed, specifics on how to handle each piece, and the American versus the continental styles of using silverware
- Dinnerware and stemware, including how to use specific pieces.

The Silverware

Silverware is used from the outside in. Work your way inward toward the plate. Whenever a course is finished, the silverware and plates or bowls will be cleared away. This serves as a clue to use the next inward piece of silverware. In a restaurant, usually a salad and entrée fork, teaspoon, and entrée knife are served at lunch. The entrée knife doubles as a salad knife. For dinner at fine restaurants, the salad knife and fish knife are added.

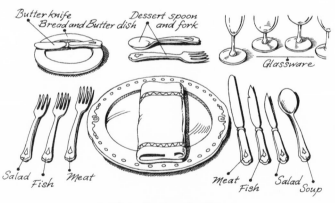

A Place Setting for Dinner

The dessert knife, fork, or spoon may already be placed on the table when you sit down or they may be placed on the dessert plate when dessert is served.

Butter Knife
Placed across the bread and butter plate, this small knife is used to serve yourself butter from the butter serving dish. It is also used to butter your bread.

Dessert Fork or Spoon
Either one or both of these utensils will be placed at the top of your plate, depending on what kind of dessert is served. These utensils may be provided at the time dessert is served rather than at the beginning of the meal.

Soup Spoon
Located farthest to the right of the knives.

Salad Fork
Usually a smaller fork, it is located on the outside on the left side of the plate.

Salad Knife

Located to the left of the soup spoon. A salad knife is not always provided and can be requested if desired.

Fish Fork

Located between the salad and meat forks.

Fish Knife

Located between the salad and entrée knives, the fish knife is designed with a point at the tip to make it useful in the removal of the backbone of the fish.

Meat or Entrée Fork

Located closest to the plate on the left, the entrée fork is usually larger than the other forks.

Meat or Entrée Knife

Located closest to the plate on the right side. This knife is usually larger than the other knives and can be used as a salad knife if one is not provided.

DIFFERENT WAYS TO USE SILVERWARE

The American Method

Put fork in left hand, using the left index finger to push the handle of the fork tines down into the food. Hold the knife with your right hand, using the index finger to make a sawing motion to cut food. After each piece is cut, lay the knife across the outer-most right-hand side of the plate with the cutting edge facing the diner. Return fork to your right hand to carry food into your mouth.

The Continental Method

Follow the same procedure except after cutting the meat, keep the fork in your left hand and put the cut food into your mouth using the left hand. The continental style is more efficient since there is no passing of the fork to and from each hand. The procedure is reversed if the diner is left-handed.

SILVERWARE PLACEMENT WHEN FINISHED EATING

Iced Tea Spoon
Place on saucer or to the right of the service plate.

Soup Spoon
Place to the right of the soup bowl on the service plate.

Salad Fork and Salad Knife
Place with fork tines facing down in the salad bowl or to the right of the bowl on the service plate.

Entrée Fork and Knife
Place with fork tines face down on the plate alongside the knife in the position shown.

Dinnerware

Service Plates

These oversized plates are placed under salad and dinner plates. They remain on the table throughout the meal with serving plates placed on top of them during each course.

Bread and Butter Plate

Placed to the left and top of the dinner plate.

Salad Plate

Placed to the left side of the dinner plate above the forks, or on top of a service plate.

Dessert Plate

Placed on the table when dessert is served.

Glassware or Stemware

Glasses are placed in a row behind the knife, starting on the left with

- Champagne
- Water
- Burgundy and
- Bordeaux.

A white wine glass may be added at the top.

This illustration shows the shapes of stemware.

2

General
Etiquette for
Dining

This section explains the general approach to dining either formally or informally:

- The exact progression of the dining experience, including time of arrival, how to use napkins and finger bowls, and the use of different wines.
- How to eat certain foods from caviar to snails.
- Common blunders and their solutions.

Before Dinner

Gifts for the Host or Hostess

You may want to take a memento to your host or hostess. It does not have to be a gift of food or drink.

Gifts can be as unique as a CD, book, or something that would have special meaning to the host or hostess. Food and liquor can present problems if intended to be used during dinner since your host or hostess has already planned what to serve. The hostess can put the gift aside for use later. Flowers must be attended to immediately, and your hostess may not have the time to spare. Sending flowers a day ahead of the party is a nice gesture. Remember, a gift does not substitute for a written thank-you note or for reciprocal entertainment.

If Arriving Early

Try not to.

If Arriving Late

Don't—but in case of a true emergency, always call ahead and inform your host or hostess of the approximate time of arrival.

If Famished before a Function

Eat a piece of fruit or snack before arriving so as not to appear to be starving.

Helping in the Kitchen

Only a particularly close friend of the host or hostess should offer to help.

Wait Staff

While at a formal dinner, if you know the wait staff, it is not appropriate to converse with them while they are serving. A simple "Hello" or "Good evening" is acceptable. If you want to engage in conversation with the staff, do so after dinner and away from the table. The wait staff is working, and conversation with them interrupts their work.

Announcing Dinner

The host or hostess walks among the guests to announce that "Dinner is served." If the party is rather large, friends of the host or hostess may assist in this procedure.

When the host or hostess announces that it is time for dinner, gather around the table, look for your place card, or wait for the host or hostess to assign you a seat.

Seating

A woman can either seat herself or wait for the man on her left to hold her chair. Men should always assist women in seating. The man assists the woman to his right.

Place Cards

Do not switch place cards in an attempt to sit in a more preferred spot. At the conclusion of the dinner, it is permissible to use cards to record names and phone numbers of the guests.

During Dinner

Guests can follow the lead of the host or hostess if unsure about how to use napkins, silverware, or glassware, or how to eat a particular type of food.

Napkins
You may place your napkin in your lap after the host or hostess has done so. Napkins are laid, unfolded, to the right of the plate when you excuse yourself from the table momentarily. Always place the napkin so that the soiled portion is facing down on the table. When you are finished with the meal, gently tap your mouth (do not vigorously wipe it), then fold the napkin casually and place to the right of your plate.

Napkin Rings
They are usually used in a private residence for a family gathering. Remove the napkin and place the ring to the left of the plate.

Saying Grace

When another person says grace, you may join in with "Amen" if you desire.

Alcohol

The host or hostess will usually offer drinks before dinner. Hard liquor should never be consumed during the meal, and drinks should not be carried to the table when dinner is announced. Do not drink more than you can tolerate. If you do not drink alcohol, feel free to ask for a nonalcoholic beverage.

DURING THE MEAL...

WHITE WINES ARE USUALLY SERVED WITH

- Soup
- Salad
- Fish
- White poultry meat.

RED WINES ARE USUALLY SERVED WITH
- Duck, pheasant, or other wild game
- Red-meat fish such as salmon or tuna
- Red meats including steak and lamb.

Champagne is usually served with dessert.

If you are at a formal dinner or restaurant and do not want the beverage that is being served, put your hand over the glass and say, "No, thank you"—or ask that it be removed. If you are at a private residence, simply say, "No, thank you."

Toasts

Toasts may be proposed by anyone, including whomever the host or hostess might select. You may propose a toast anytime during the dinner. Usually the person delivering the toast stands, followed by all other guests rising except the one being honored. After the toast, everyone except the one being toasted sips from a wine glass (or water glass if a person does not drink alcohol). The person being toasted merely picks up a wine glass and gestures and waits until everyone has sipped to the toast. Do not sip from your glass if you are the one being toasted.

Serving Yourself

When different bowls of food are directly in front of you, take a bowl, offer it to the person on your left, then to the right, then serve yourself and pass the bowl to your right.

Second Helpings

At a formal lunch or dinner with multiple courses, second helpings are not usually offered. If they are offered, then it is perfectly appropriate to serve yourself a second helping.

Cleaning Your Plate

Do not soak up the gravy or sauce with bread and try to get every last morsel off your plate and into your mouth. Your plate should not appear as though it has been washed. It is always proper to leave a bite or two on your plate.

Crumbs

At a formal dinner where wait staff serve, table crumbs should be removed by the staff.

Any soft crumb, such as butter or sauce, can be quietly removed by the guest with an eating utensil and then placed on the side of the plate. At fine restaurants, the wait person will use a miniature silver-handled broom and a silver-handled dustpan to "crumb" the table. A wait person can also use a scraper, resembling a small curved ruler with a handle, to clear the table of crumbs.

Dropped Napkin

In a private residence, pick up the napkin. You may either continue using it or request another one. At a restaurant, ask for a replacement.

Dropped Silverware on Floor

Always ask for a replacement. Do not bend down searching for your lost utensil.

Spilled Drink or Food

If you spill something, do not make a scene. Simply murmur a small apology and let the host, hostess, or wait staff take care of it. It is not acceptable for guests to clean up the spill. It creates havoc if everyone tries to help. If you spill something while dining at a private residence, offer to send the tablecloth to a good dry cleaner. Then pick up the cloth later and return it as soon as possible to the host or hostess.

Finger Bowls

The finger bowl is filled one-third full with warm water. A small doily is placed under the bowl, and the bowl is served on a dessert plate. Usually finger bowls are provided at state dinners or other formal events.

PROCEDURE:

- You may squeeze lemon into the water if you have eaten fish.
- Dip fingers into water.
- Tap wet fingers on your lips to clean them.
- Tap your napkin on your lips to dry them.
- Dry fingers on napkin.

- Move the finger bowl and doily to a position just behind the dessert plate and a little to the left.
- Do not leave finger bowl on the dessert plate.

ADVICE: If there are no finger bowls and you need water to clean your fingers, you may rub them around a cold glass to moisten with condensation. Then gently wipe your damp fingers on a napkin. Do this casually so no one notices.

Damp Cloths

Damp cloths can be served after eating difficult foods, such as lobsters and crabs. Sometimes they are warmed in a microwave. Unfold the damp cloth and wipe your hands off. When finished cleaning hands and fingers, place the damp cloths on a tray for removal. Never place them directly on a table after use.

Smoking

Do not smoke in a private residence. If you must smoke, step outside. By doing so, you are being considerate of the host or hostess, as well as other guests.

Elbows and Hands

Do not spread elbows out like wings on an airplane while eating. You can put elbows on the table between courses and when the table is cleared of dishes. Otherwise, keep the idle arm off the table while you are eating by placing it in your lap. If you do place elbows on the table between courses, be sure they do not take up the space of the person seated next to you.

HOW TO EAT CERTAIN FOODS

Breads
A small butter knife is usually located on the butter plate.

- Using the butter knife, take about a teaspoon of butter from the butter dish and place it onto your butter plate.
- Break off a small piece of bread and butter it for eating, using the butter from your plate.
- It is acceptable to butter an entire piece of bread if it is served hot so that the butter can melt into the bread.

HINTS TO REMEMBER: Never take butter from the serving dish and put it directly onto your bread. The butter knife is used only for buttering the bread. It should not be used to cut the bread in half. When tearing French bread or breaking a roll, pull the bread apart gently. Since French bread can pull apart suddenly, your elbow can land in your neighbor's mouth.

Caviar

Place a couple of teaspoons of caviar on your plate and squeeze lemon juice over it. Spread caviar onto small pieces of toast. You may top with minced, hard-boiled egg yolk, minced onions, and sour cream if desired; however, these embellishments can interfere with the luxurious taste of caviar.

Clams and oysters

For clams or oysters served on the half shell…

- Hold shell firmly with one hand and use a fork to remove the oyster or clam.
- Dip the oyster or clam in a sauce and eat in one bite.
- Some enjoy drinking the remaining juice from the clam shell. (Imagine the picture you present before doing so.)

While lemon juice enhances the taste of oysters and clams, some clam and oyster aficionados contend that the tomato-based sauces often served with these dishes smother the luscious seafood taste.

Usually steamed clams are served on a plate, along with a small container of melted butter and a cup of hot clam broth. For these types of clams...

- Spread the partially opened clam shell with the thumb and forefinger of your left hand.
- Then use the thumb, index, and second finger on your right hand to pull out the clam body.
- Take off the clam sheath and discard into the communal bowl on the table.
- Dip clam into broth or melted butter.
- It is acceptable to drink the clam juice but be aware of your image while doing so.
- After clams are served, finger bowls are usually provided. (See finger bowls, pages 24 and 50)

Condiments

Always spoon jams and jellies onto the bread and butter plate. If you do not have a bread and butter plate, spoon the condiments onto your dinner plate and then spread some of the condiments onto your bread. Never spoon butter, jams, or jellies directly onto a roll from a serving dish. In the same manner, place cranberry or horseradish sauce onto your plate first, not directly onto the meat.

Crab

Request a bib at a restaurant because the process can become quite messy. First take the legs off and siphon out the meat as if the legs were straws. Turn the crab on its back and pick out the meat with a nutpick or oyster fork. Crack open the claws with a nutcracker to retrieve meat.

Fish

If the fish is served with its head and tail, cut off both before you start to eat the fish. Place the head and tail on a plate that is provided. Use the very wide knife to cut the fish away from the skeleton. You may lift the backbone by using the tines of your fork and discard it, along with the head and tail, on the provided plate. Do not put the bones on your bread and butter plate. If no plate is provided, request one.

Hors d'Oeuvres

If the serving platter is for everyone at the table, take a portion from the platter and put it on your own small plate. Do not eat directly from the serving platter.

Lobster

If the lobster is not already cut away from the shell, request a bib, because eating lobster can be a messy venture. The following steps tell how to prepare and eat it...

- Twist off the front claws and crack them open with a nutcracker.
- Remove meat with a nutpick or oyster fork.
- Break the tail off from the body. You can usually cut up the tail meat with a knife and fork.
- The legs of the lobster can be broken off and the insides eaten by siphoning them like a straw.
- Cut the soft undershell from the hard outer shell with a knife along the seam on both sides. Simply peel the undershell away; meat is then ex-

posed and can be cut out and eaten.

• Never use tip of a knife to spear the meat and place in your mouth.

1. Twist off large claws.

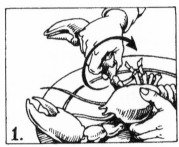

2. Crack claws with nutcracker.

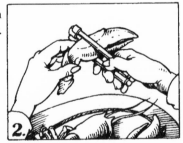

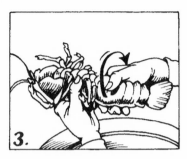

3. Hold back and twist to remove tail section.

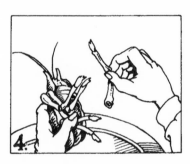

4. Break off legs and siphon meat out as if using a straw.

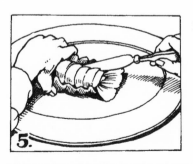

5. Cut soft undershell from the hard outershell with knife along the seam on both sides and peel undershell away.

Picante Sauce and Chips

Spoon a portion of picante sauce onto the small plate provided and then scoop the sauce up with your chip. Do not scoop your chip through the main serving bowl.

Salads

The salad fork is the outermost fork on your left. If salad leaves are too large, cut them with a knife, then rest the knife on your salad plate. Cutting is preferred over trying to stuff large leaves into your mouth. When finished, lay the fork and knife either to the right on the service plate, or lay knife and fork diagonally facing down on the salad plate.

Shrimp

First, take off the legs underneath the shrimp. This will expose a place to easily grasp the shell. Pull off the shell with one movement. Run the tines of your fork down the back of the shrimp to remove the vein. You can either use the tail to dip the shrimp into sauce—or remove the tail, spear the shrimp with your fork and dip. Squeeze the tail gently to remove the meat from the tail. You may dip shrimp in the sauce between each bite as long as it is your own sauce dish. Do not dip into a serving dish—instead scoop some sauce onto your plate and dip. Deposit shrimp shells in a communal dish or on the side of your plate.

Snails

Special tongs called snail grippers are provided to grasp each snail, as well as a snail fork to remove the snail from its shell. If a snail gripper is not available, use your napkin to hold the hot, buttery snail. Extract the meat with either the tiny fork or a nutpick. After the shells have cooled, they can be picked up and the juice swallowed quietly. A second method of retrieving the juice from the snail shells is to turn the snail over, empty the juice onto your plate, blot it up with some pieces of bread, and retrieve the bread with a fork.

The garlic butter remaining in the dish may be eaten by dropping small pieces of bread into the sauce and eating with a fork; however, remember not to appear to gobble up every last drop.

Sorbet
Sorbet is a fruit ice that looks like sherbet. It is usually served on an orange slice, and contains about two or three teaspoons. Its purpose is to cleanse the palate, usually after the salad. Eat sorbet with the small spoon that accompanies the small plate and small bowl. Eat only one or two teaspoons. Do not eat the orange slice nor the lettuce and other garnishes surrounding the sorbet.

Soup
When soup is the first course, it may be set in place before or after guests are seated. Usually the soup bowl is served already filled. A large, round soup spoon is placed either at the right of the knife or supplied with the soup.

Take soup spoon, dip into bowl. Drag spoon away from you to edge of bowl. Rest spoon on edge for a moment so it will not drip. Bring spoon up to mouth.

You may tilt the bowl away from you to get the last bit of soup. When finished, place your soup spoon on the service plate to the right of the bowl.

SOLUTIONS TO COMMON BLUNDERS

DO NOT:

DO:

Push food onto fork with your fingers or your bread.

Use your knife to push food onto fork, or use your fork to spear the food.

Pick your teeth with toothpick or tines of fork.

Use your tongue discreetly to dislodge food from a tooth, or excuse yourself to the powder room to take care of the problem.

Clean your teeth with your napkin.

Go to the powder room— teeth are never cleaned in public.

Blow your nose on a napkin.

You may dab your nose discreetly if it bothers you, then excuse yourself to the powder room and solve the problem.

Talk with your mouth full.

If asked a question while your mouth is full, chew and swallow before answering.

DO NOT:	DO:
Reach across the table for an item.	Ask to have it passed to you.
Burp out loud.	Cover your mouth with a napkin to stifle sound. If burping continues, excuse yourself and go to powder room.
Eat directly off someone's plate.	Ask for two plates so you can divide the portion and place onto separate plates.
Order items that are unfamiliar.	Ask for interpretation.
Say you dislike a food that is being served.	Say nothing critical— decline with a smile and say, "No, thank you."
Yell out if you find a piece of foreign matter in the food.	Either don't eat the food, or ask that you receive another serving.
Spit out a fish or chicken bone directly onto the plate.	Deposit the unwanted food, bone, or other item on the tines of a fork and then discard on your

DO NOT:	DO:
	plate to the left of food that you are eating.
Leave spoon in glass of iced tea or cup of coffee.	Rest the spoon on the beverage serving plate. If there is none, request a small plate.
Leave tea bag in cup.	Place on saucer next to cup or ask for a small plate on which to place the bag.
Drink coffee or tea from your saucer if the liquid spills.	Simply leave liquid in the saucer, or take cup off saucer and pour the liquid back into the cup.
Refresh or apply lipstick, comb hair, or perform grooming tasks at the table.	Visit the powder room for all touch-ups.

3

How to Be a Gracious Host or Hostess

This section illustrates and discusses how a host or hostess can entertain flawlessly in a private residence. Topics include:

- What to do before and during dinner
- How to seat guests
- How to recover if a guest spills something
- What to do if a guest asks to smoke
- Other tips for the host and hostess.

Preparation before Entertaining

Help in the Kitchen

Decide what needs to be done and whether or not you will need to hire some help. Make a list for the staff and yourself to keep things running smoothly. Prepare your staff for what is expected of them throughout the entire evening. Compliment them as the evening progresses. Do not enlist or accept help from guests unless they are very close friends.

Dietary Needs

Ask each guest about dietary needs so alternate dishes can be prepared to ensure against conflicts with religious beliefs and medical difficulties.

Smoking

Decide what you will do if someone asks to smoke. It is acceptable for smokers to step outside while smoking. Other guests appreciate this gesture. Some may be allergic to smoke of any kind. It is best to know in advance how to handle this situation and ask politely that guests smoke outside. Prepare a smoking area on a patio or deck equipped with table, tablecloth, chairs, and ashtrays—so your smoking guests will not feel like outcasts.

Drinks

Have a designated area to serve drinks. Offer sparkling water and soft drinks in addition to any alcoholic beverages.

Place for Coats and Umbrellas

Designate a specific place, such as the front hall closet or a bed, where guests may store their wraps.

Seating

If you are the host or hostess, you may seat individuals where they will enjoy one another. A guest of honor or the host or hostess can sit at either end of the table. It is not necessary to follow a woman/man seating plan all around the table. Two or three women or men may sit next to one another.

Left-Handed Guests

Seat left-handed people at a corner or in a position where they will not be bumping into their right-handed neighbors all evening.

Place Cards

Use place cards when ten or more people are invited. Place the card behind the plate next to the glasses. When preparing place cards, always write first and last names. Always place your guests who do not know other guests on either side of you. Handwritten menus, which are also put behind the plate, are sometimes presented at large formal events.

If you do not have place cards, make a mental note in advance where you want everyone to sit in order to expedite the seating.

Late Arrivals

If a guest does not call to tell you he or she will be late, wait only for a few minutes, then serve as planned. Some guests may not call at all, and your dinner could be indefinitely delayed.

Dinner Is Served

Guests will watch the host or hostess to determine what to do with unfamiliar foods and eating utensils; therefore you should begin eating as soon as everyone is served.

Announcing Dinner
The host or hostess should walk around to guests and announce, "Dinner is served." If the party is rather large, close friends can assist in this procedure.

Saying Grace
Whether or not to say grace is left to the discretion of the host or hostess. If you would like a guest to say grace, invite that person to do so. Be aware, however, that the request might very well make your guest uncomfortable, so you may want to ask privately ahead of time.

Toasts

If you wish to honor a guest, you may propose a toast or select someone else to propose one. Other guests may wish to propose additional toasts. (For more specifics about toasts see pages 21-22.)

Serving Food

You or your staff initiate the serving of all food. For informal dinners, take a bowl, hold it for your guest to the left, then to the right; then serve yourself and pass the bowl to your right.

Napkins

By placing the napkin in your lap, you signal guests that it is time to do the same and begin.

Napkin Rings

Napkin rings are usually used in private residences for family gatherings only. If you choose to use napkin rings, remove the napkin and place the ring to the left of your plate on the table.

Spilled Drink or Food

If a guest accidentally spills something, remain calm. Dab the area with a cloth and tell the individual not to worry. Otherwise, act as if nothing had happened. Your composure keeps the tone of the party calm and prevents interruption of the flow of conversation. Have clean, fresh cloths available in case of spills.

Second Helpings

When a guest takes a second helping, you must serve yourself at least a small second helping if your plate is empty or close to empty to keep that guest from feeling uncomfortable.

Clearing the Plates Between Courses

Clear plates only after the last person has finished eating. Take the plates away two at a time. It is not appropriate to scrape the plates at the table and then clear them. For a formal dinner, services should be removed by staff at the end of each course.

Dropped Napkin or Silverware

When a guest drops a napkin, offer a replacement. Have extra napkins and silverware available in case one is dropped. When a guest drops silverware, replace it immediately. Do not allow a guest to search for the lost utensil on the floor.

Crumbs

When giving a formal dinner with wait staff, instruct them to crumb the table between courses. It is not necessary to crumb the table if no staff is available.

Finger Bowls

If serving messy foods, such as lobster, clams, or even corn on the cob, be sure to include finger bowls or damp cloths. Always allow your guests some means of cleaning their hands or fingers. Remove the finger bowls after the guests are finished.

Damp Cloths

If you want to try something new, try the oriental idea of damp cloths provided to guests—usually at the end of the entrée. The cloths are served after eating difficult foods, such as lobsters and crabs. Scented damp cloths can interfere with the wonderful aromas of the food. An easy way to heat damp cloths is by putting them in the microwave.

Complicated Foods

When serving foods difficult to eat, such as lobster or unpeeled shrimp, be aware that a guest may not know how to eat a particular dish. You should eat slowly so that a guest can follow your lead. If a particularly unusual dish is served and the setting is relaxed, then it may even be enjoyable to give a demonstration to all the guests and turn the meal into an adventure.

Remember, as host or hostess, you should continue eating until the last guest finishes to prevent anyone from feeling uncomfortable.

Hints On Entertaining

- Eat something before the party to help maintain your energy and equanimity throughout the evening.
- Be an example of good etiquette for your guests.
- Your mood will set the tone. Be cheerful, interested and, no matter what happens, relaxed.
- If children are present, set aside a room for them to play safely. This will calm anxious parents.
- Always entertain within your means. Guests come to your party to enjoy one another's company.
- Have fun!

4

Dining and Entertaining at Restaurants

This section explains the details of dining and entertaining at a restaurant. Topics include:

- The benefits of restaurant entertaining
- How to handle reservations and paying the bill
- How to order food
- When to ask for a doggy bag
- Other tips for restaurant dining.

Benefits of Restaurant Entertaining

The major benefit of entertaining at a restaurant or club is the lack of preparation before the event. This type of entertaining requires no shopping, no cooking, no staff, and no clean-up afterward.

General Etiquette for Dining at Restaurants

Reservations

The person who issues the invitation should make the reservation and pick up the check. The following guidelines will assume that a host or hostess will make the arrangements and pay for the dinner. If you are the host or hostess, arrange for paying the bill when you make reservations, but pay the bill after the function. This allows you to tip accordingly.

Appropriate Dress Codes

Ask about a dress code. You must make your guests, both men and women, aware if the restaurant or club has a dress code. Often the restaurant provides men's coats and ties for those inappropriately dressed, but you will prefer to spare your guests this embarrassment and the discomfort of an ill-fitting jacket.

First to Arrive

If you arrive before your host or hostess, you may either wait or ask to be seated at the reserved table.

Late Arrivals

Whether you are alone or with others, wait fifteen minutes before ordering if a member of your party has not arrived. If you are a guest running late, call the restaurant and leave word for the host or hostess and give an estimated time of arrival so that the meal can begin without you.

Checking Wraps
Check wraps, topcoats, hats, and umbrellas when dining at a restaurant.

Cocktails
Hard-liquor beverages are served before dinner and never during dinner. Diners who do not drink alcoholic beverages should drink water or request a non-alcoholic beverage.

Wait Staff
They are there to wait on you—not to be your friends. Do not visit with them.

Seating
Upon your arrival, you may either wait for your party or ask to be seated. If you are the host or hostess and do not like the table or seating area where your party has been placed, ask politely for another desired area. Do this before guests arrive to prevent embarrassment and confusion.

If you are the first to arrive for a dutch-treat lunch or dinner, ask to be seated in a desirable spot. This is usually away from the traffic of the kitchen, cashier, and maître d' station.

Napkins

At fine restaurants, the maître d' will place the napkin in your lap. Do not use the napkin as a bib. If during the meal you drop your napkin on the floor, ask for a replacement.

If the napkin is not placed in your lap, the host will place the napkin in his lap, which serves as a clue for the other diners to do the same. If there is no host or hostess, place the napkin in your lap as soon as you are seated.

Napkin Rings

Napkin rings are not used in fine dining establishments.

How to Order at a Restaurant

The maître d' will take your order for cocktails first. When your drinks come, you may ask the serving person to wait for five to ten minutes before taking your order.

When it comes time to order your entrée, the person on the right of the host or hostess orders first. If you have not made your selections when it comes your turn to order, ask for another moment. Remember, do not order the most expensive item on the menu. If you are a guest, it is considered thoroughly rude and thoughtless to do this, even if the meal is being paid for by a company as a business expense. If you want something not on the menu, ask if it is available.

Poorly Prepared Food
If food is served cold or improperly cooked, ask the waiter to make the adjustment, either by heating, cooking longer, or replacing it.

Complaints

If a serving person mistakenly gives you the wrong order, quietly point that out. Do not yell or make a scene. Under no circumstances should you use questionable language to register a complaint at any time. It is not correct to eat food that is not yours. If you do eat someone else's entrée, it can cause real problems for the chef and wait staff.

Ordering Dessert

Never order more than one dessert. If you do not want an entire dessert, just eat what you want. Do not sample a dessert from another person's plate. Request two plates if you want to split a dessert.

Doggy Bags

If you are eating with family members, you may ask for a doggy bag. If you are entertaining or are a guest, it is not proper to ask for a doggy bag.

Paying the Check

If you are the host or hostess, make arrangements in advance to pay the bill after dinner. Never allow a hassle to take place over the check. If the check is to be paid dutch treat, discuss the arrangements beforehand and have enough cash on hand to pay for it quickly. Fine restaurants will not give separate checks.

Tipping

It is customary to tip 15 percent of the total bill. Ask if service is included because many restaurants now include the tip in the total bill. Tipping above 15 percent for exceptional service is acceptable and appreciated. You may also want to tip the bus persons.

Smoking

You may smoke in a designated smoking area but only before and after dinner—not during the meal.

5

Dining at Meetings, Parties, and Luxurious Places

This section illustrates and discusses:

- How to conduct business while dining
- Which foods to avoid at business meals
- What to expect at parties—from tailgate parties to formal teas
- What to expect when dining at luxurious places, such as limousines and yachts.

Conducting Business Meals

Size of Table

Be sure that the size of the table will accommodate the guests plus their paper work and tablets, as well as the food.

Talking before Ordering

Tell the wait person that you want five or ten minutes before you order. To ensure that everyone has time to finish eating before the meeting ends, do not wait too long before ordering. It is easy to get caught up in the meeting and completely forget the meal. Then your business colleagues may leave hungry.

Ordering Food

Since business meals should be relaxed and productive, order food that is easy to eat and manageable. It is difficult to eat large pieces of salad leaves and slurp long strings of sauce-covered spaghetti. If you were to see yourself in a mirror while eating such foods, you would be appalled. So order bite-sized salads and easy-to-eat soups and entrées.

Alcoholic Beverages

Never order wine or other alcoholic drinks at a business meeting if your host or hostess refrains from doing so. In fact, it is best not to drink at all while doing business. During dinner, one drink may be acceptable but none is better. Keep in mind the kind of impression you want to make. You will make it better with a clear head.

Telephone

Your cellular telephone should only be used away from the dining table and only in an absolute emergency. Often viewed as a power game, using your personal telephone during the meal insults your dining companions. Excuse yourself to make calls only if the calls cannot possibly wait.

Beepers

If a beeper or pager is absolutely necessary, turn down the ring. If your beeper goes off, excuse yourself only for the calls of the utmost importance. Beepers can also be viewed as a power game unless you are a physician or one who deals with emergency situations.

Dining in the Boardroom

Order a fixed menu with one or two main foods in advance of the meeting. It takes too long to have everyone order something different, and payment becomes cumbersome.

Types of Parties

Beach Party

If you are invited to a private beach club, check with your host or hostess about whether to bring your own towel and other beach gear. You should also find out if you should pay (or will need to pay) for the food and drinks that you order. Always bring something modest to wear over your swimsuit. Many clubs will not allow you in their dining rooms, or even their outside buffet areas, if you are wearing just a swimsuit. Most clubs have a snack bar where you can get hamburgers or a casual meal, but even that part of the club might require a cover-up. Ask your host or hostess about appropriate attire.

Buffet Parties

Always allow everyone to finish the salad before you go to a buffet table for your entrée. Do not load up your plate with mounds of food that you will not eat.

Picnics

The most familiar picnics might include food served on paper plates. Picnics can also be elegant affairs, with linen-covered tables, long-stemmed wine glasses, fragile china, and sterling silver. Attire for such an occasion is much different than the usual blue jeans and T-shirt you expect to wear when invited to a picnic. Always ask the host or hostess about the proper dress.

Cocktail Parties

Deposit pits, seeds, bones or really tough meat in a cocktail napkin and discard them in a wastepaper basket. To protect your dignity, anticipate what might happen when eating certain party foods. For example, small tomatoes can burst forth like a seed shower onto the person standing nearby if you put the entire tomato in your mouth and bite down. Do not go to a cocktail party and eat as though it were a dinner. Do not load up your plate with mounds of food. If hungry, eat a snack before arriving at the party. Once at the party, eat one or two hors d'oeuvres and visit and enjoy the other guests.

Tailgate Parties

A tailgate party can be as simple an event as lowering the tailgate of a truck for use as a table, or as elaborate as hiring a chef to bring a catering trailer on site to barbecue your favorite meat. Some tailgate parties involve luxury RVs or limousines with silver flasks and fine china. Again, check with your host or hostess about appropriate attire.

Usually these parties occur at football or baseball games and other sporting events. Some parties serve food that signifies the opposing team's mascot, such as beef for the University of Texas Longhorns.

Debutante Teas

Traditionally, only women are invited to this very formal occasion held in the afternoon. It is now becoming more common to include men. You should expect to be greeted by a receiving line. It is nice to send flowers to the young debutante the day before the party.

A tea dance is held later in the day. It is appropriate for male guests to ask both the mother and the young debutante for a dance at least once during the evening. Drinks and hors d'oeuvres will be served on trays by waiters.

Formal Teas

You may think of this as a strictly English tradition, but it is actually very common to find formal teas occurring in the United States. A tea usually takes place in the afternoon and is a great occasion to meet people. Coffee is also served. Guests are expected to serve themselves after the host or hostess has served them the first cup of tea or coffee. Around the room should be different plates of food, such as cucumber or salmon sandwiches, from which guests are expected to serve themselves. A tea is usually held in a very formal room with places to sit and stand. Formal tea is served at finer restaurants and hotels from 2:00 P.M. until around 5:00 P.M.

High Tea

In America "high tea" is often interchanged with the more correct term of "formal tea." In England and other European countries, high tea describes a tea served from 4:00 P.M. until early evening at local pubs. The clientele serve themselves rather large portions of food piled high on small plates and drink hot tea.

Luxurious Places to Dine

Corporate Jet

The size of the aircraft determines the type of service offered to guests. In larger aircraft, a flight attendant will serve you. Treat the flight attendant as you would any wait person, except that it is not appropriate to tip. A corporation will often have the day's newspapers from all over the world available. Food can be served on fine china, crystal, and silverware, all bearing the corporate logo. Usually the lunch or dinner is not a formal affair.

Limousine

Often limousines will have a refrigerator for snacks and beverages. When you order your limousine, you will order champagne and other food. If there is anything else that you need, you can always ask the chauffeur. Always make sure that the limousine is stopped before you pour a drink.

On a Cruise

When booking passage on a cruise, reserve your table in the dining room. There are two sittings that you can choose for meals—early or late. If you are dining alone, ask to be seated at a miscellaneous table. This will give you an opportunity to meet other people who are alone on the cruise.

If you want to throw a bon voyage party, you must first get permission from the cruise line. Make sure such a party is permitted. If so, arrange with the steward to have soft drinks, glasses, and hors d'oeuvres furnished at your expense. Since cruise ships are not allowed to sell liquor while in port, you will have to furnish your own liquor. Make sure that you do your part in helping your friends off the ship when it comes time for them to go. Once you are out at sea, if you want to have a cocktail party, you will only have to pay for the liquor.

The first thing you should do, once on board, is to go directly to the purser and reconfirm your dining room reservation. If while on board you are honored by being invited to eat at the Captain's Table, accept the offer immediately and appreciatively. You should never try to have yourself invited, even to an officer's table. You should address the captain as "Captain" followed by his surname. Other officers on the ship are called "Mister."

At lunch, men wear jackets and ties, unless the lunch is served buffet style on deck, in which case they may dress informally. Women may wear summer dresses in the dining room and slacks or shorts on deck. As for tipping, each individual ship line should send you a flier informing you of the tipping procedures to follow on board that ship.

Out on a Powerboat

Dining on a runabout or powerboat can be a lot of fun. A picnic is the usual fare. Always ask your host or hostess what clothes to wear. It is important to obey the captain and follow orders, as he or she is responsible for everyone's life on board. Do not discard dining rubbish into the water.

Train

On a train, you eat in the dining car, which like a cruise has two seating times. You can make arrangements with the maître d' after you have already boarded the train, and he will assign you a table. The dining car is open to all who are traveling on the train. Tip the personnel in the dining car as you would in a restaurant—15 percent and more for extraordinary service.

Yacht

Dining on a yacht can be quite elegant. Lunch is usually served buffet style. Dinner can be either formal or casual. Dine as you would in a fine restaurant.

Depending on the size of the vessel, a chef can prepare the most superb meals imaginable. In fact, some yacht owners hire renowned chefs to prepare their specialities for special occasions. Reading the guidelines about dining etiquette described in the previous chapters of this book will enable you to relax while on board and enjoy whatever is served.

While on board a yacht, you should tip the crew as you would in a luxury hotel. If the owner is not on board, it is appropriate to bring the Captain a gift since he is then considered the host. You should tip the stewards between ten and twenty dollars each, depending on how much service they rendered.

Now you are ready to dine with confidence.
Enjoy!

As my grandmother says—
"You cannot have two sets of manners!"

ABOUT THE AUTHOR

Sheila M. Long is the CEO of Long's International Trainers Bureau, a corporation that furnishes trainers and consultants to *Fortune* 100 companies. As a corporate trainer herself, Mrs. Long has developed and delivered numerous cutting-edge seminars to her clients.